A GREAT G...

CHESS

BY MARISSA BOLTE

Norwood House Press

For information regarding Norwood House Press, please visit our website at www.norwoodhousepress.com or call 866-565-2900.

Credits
Editor: Kristy Stark
Designer: Sara Radka
Fact Checker: Stephanie Loureiro & Ann Schwab

Photo Credits
Getty Images: Allsport/John Gichigi, 25, Chess Club and Scholastic Center of Saint Louis/Ilya S. Savenok, 29, Chris Hondros, 33, Dilip Vishwanat, 36, Fox Photos/Harry Todd, 23, HarjeetSinghNarang, 9, John D. Buffington, 5, Mario Tama, 30, 40, michellegibson, 20, Nenov, 15, Pictorial Parade, 35, Ratchapoom Anupongpan , cover, 1, sarote pruksachat, 16, Spencer Platt, 39, Stock Ninja Studio, 15, vesnyanka, 6, Wavebreakmedia, 43; maciej326, 8, OpenClipart-Vectors, 4, 5, 15, 32, 38; Shutterstock: Anusorn Nakdee, 3, kamomeen, 13, Lennox Wright, 42, Oleg Golovnev, 19, RPBaiao, 7, T photography, 31; The Metropolitan Museum of Art: 10; Wikimedia: SP, 17, Ygrek, 26

Library of Congress Cataloging-in-Publication Data
Names: Bolte, Mari, author.
Title: Chess / By Mari Bolte.
Description: Chicago : Norwood House Press, [2022] | Series: A great game! | Includes index. | Audience: Ages 8-10 | Audience: Grades 4-6 | Summary: "An introductory look at the game of Chess. Describes the history of the game, introduces the creators and innovators, highlights competitions, and provides insight about the game's future. Informational text for readers who are new to Chess, or are interested in learning more. Includes a glossary, index, and bibliography for further reading"— Provided by publisher.
Identifiers: LCCN 2021019582 (print) | LCCN 2021019583 (ebook) | ISBN 9781684508327 (hardcover) | ISBN 9781684046461 (paperback) | ISBN 9781684046508 (epub)
Subjects: LCSH: Chess—Juvenile literature.
Classification: LCC GV1446 .B58 2022 (print) | LCC GV1446 (ebook) | DDC 794.1—dc23
LC record available at https://lccn.loc.gov/2021019582
LC ebook record available at https://lccn.loc.gov/2021019583

Hardcover ISBN: 978-1-68450-832-7
Paperback ISBN: 978-1-68404-646-1

PO339N—082021
Manufactured in the United States of America in North Mankato, Minnesota.

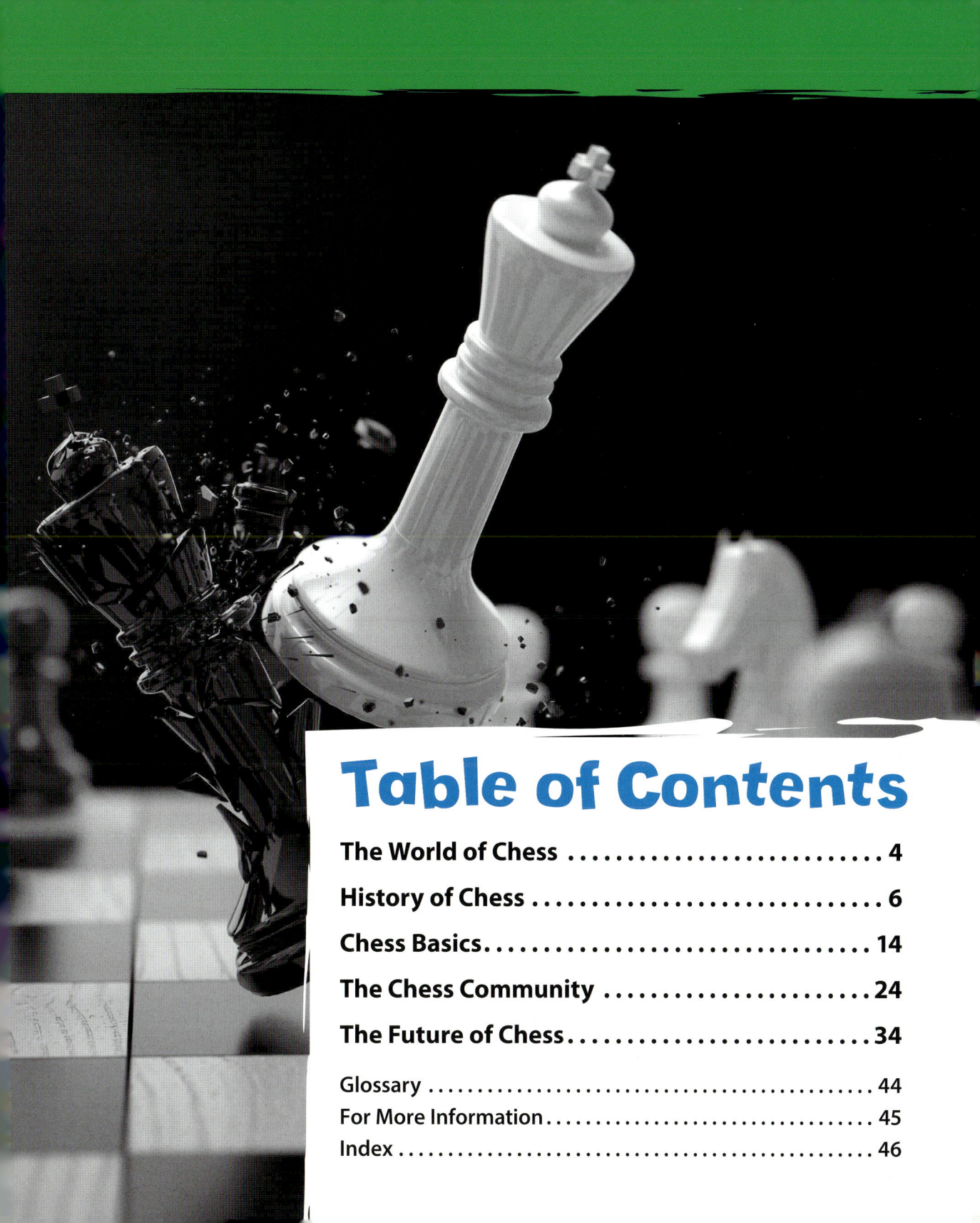

Table of Contents

The World of Chess

It's a Saturday evening and you're surrounded by friends. It is game night, and someone brings out a chess set.

Now it is your turn. It feels like every person is holding his or her breath. Your pawn slides across the board. You take your hand off the piece. It was a clever move, and your friends cheer!

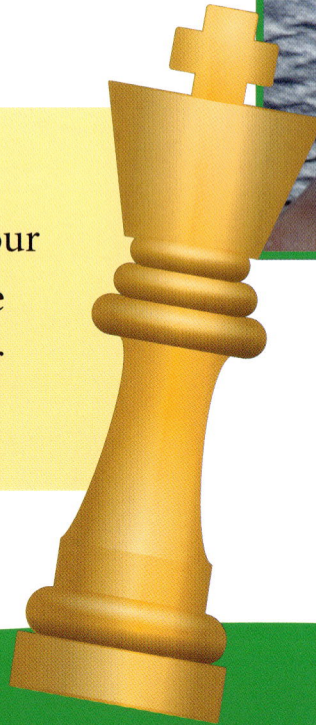

Now you wait to see what your opponent will do. Can you think far enough ahead to win the game? This is the world of chess.

History of Chess

Chess has been around for hundreds of years. Nobody knows when the game was first played. Experts can't even agree where chess started. China, India, Russia, and Pakistan are all possible places.

What they can agree on is that the game is old. It dates back to at least 501–600 CE. Historians have found writings from around this time that talk about the game. They think it is even older than that, though. After all, people were writing about a game they already knew.

DID YOU KNOW?

Chess is an old game. But there are older board games, including one called Go. Go is also a strategy game. It is more than 4,000 years old.

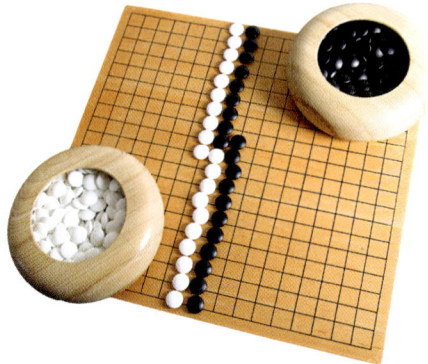

Some of the oldest chess pieces in the world are on display at the British Museum.

A game called chaturanga was an early version of chess. It was a game that was popular in India in the sixth and seventh centuries. Both games give each player 16 pieces to play with. And like chess, those pieces move in different ways. The game isn't over until the king is captured. And both games are played on a board with 64 squares.

Game rules varied on where the game was played. Chess moved east from India. It reached China by 800 CE. Buddhist monks who traveled from India probably brought the game with them. In Chinese chess, pieces are placed where lines meet, not in squares. The board was a little bigger, and the pieces were a little different.

Japan took the game and made it their own. Shogi is played on a slightly larger board with 20 pieces. Pieces can rejoin the game and play for the opposite team.

Moving the Pieces

Travelers spread the game of chess across the globe. Muslims brought it to Africa, Italy, and Spain. Viking invaders had chessboards when they conquered Iceland and England. Traders carried the game to Russia.

Like chess, chaturanga pieces depict two armies.

History of Chess: Time Line

501–600 CE
The first known writings about chess appear. Historians believe this means chess was already a known game.

Early 700s CE
Chess reaches Spain. It was probably introduced by the Moors.

800 CE
The first reference to Chinese chess appears in a book. The game was probably brought by Buddhist monks who visited India.

1500s
New chess rules are invented to make games faster.

1924
The International Chess Federation (FIDE) is founded.

1991
The oldest chess piece known to man was discovered. The piece dates back to a time between 680 and 749 CE.

The game moved west too. Muslim conquerors called the Moors probably brought it there. It was first played in Spain in the early 700s CE. A duke introduced living chess in 735 CE. Living chess was played on a giant board. People dressed in costumes represented each piece. Other stories about rulers playing living chess exist across the European continent.

Scientists are learning more about the game from ancient pieces. One was found in Jordan in 1991. The 1,300-year-old rook is less than one inch (2.5 centimeters) tall. It is made of sandstone.

In 2002, a piece made of ivory was found in Albania. It dates back to 465 CE. It might be the oldest piece found anywhere in the world.

Perhaps the most famous chess set in history is the Lewis Chessmen. They were found on the Isle of Lewis, in Scotland. They date back to 1140 to 1200. They are made out of walrus ivory and whale teeth. They have been called "Ivory Vikings."

The board changed along with the pieces. The checked board was invented in Europe around 1100. The first folding board was invented in 1125.

DID YOU KNOW?

Many terms in chess come from Persian words. For example, *shah* means "king" in Persian. *Shah mat* means "the king is frozen." Say it aloud. Then say, "**Checkmate!**" Sound similar?

Chess only continued to grow. Nobility across Europe was expected to learn how to play. Kings sponsored their favorite players. The first book about chess in English came out in 1474.

By the 1500s, chess was shaping into the game we know today. At the time, games could last hours, or even days. Rules were made to speed things along. Everyone agreed to follow them. And people started thinking more about **chess theory.**

Chess became a way of everyday life. Fans started forming and joining chess clubs. The first formal chess clubs were formed in the 1800s. Official tournaments brought top competitors together. Playing blindfolded became popular. Game clocks started making games faster. **Grandmasters** were born. People love chess!

Chess Is a War Game

The game of chess is often compared to warfare. The difference is that, in regular chess, you can see all the pieces on the board. In the late 19th century, members of the German military invented a new form of chess called Kriegspiel. It was played with three boards. Each player had their own board that only they could see. A referee kept track of all the moves on a third board.

Chess pieces are called white and black, even if they are not exactly those colors. Usually there is a dark color and a light color.

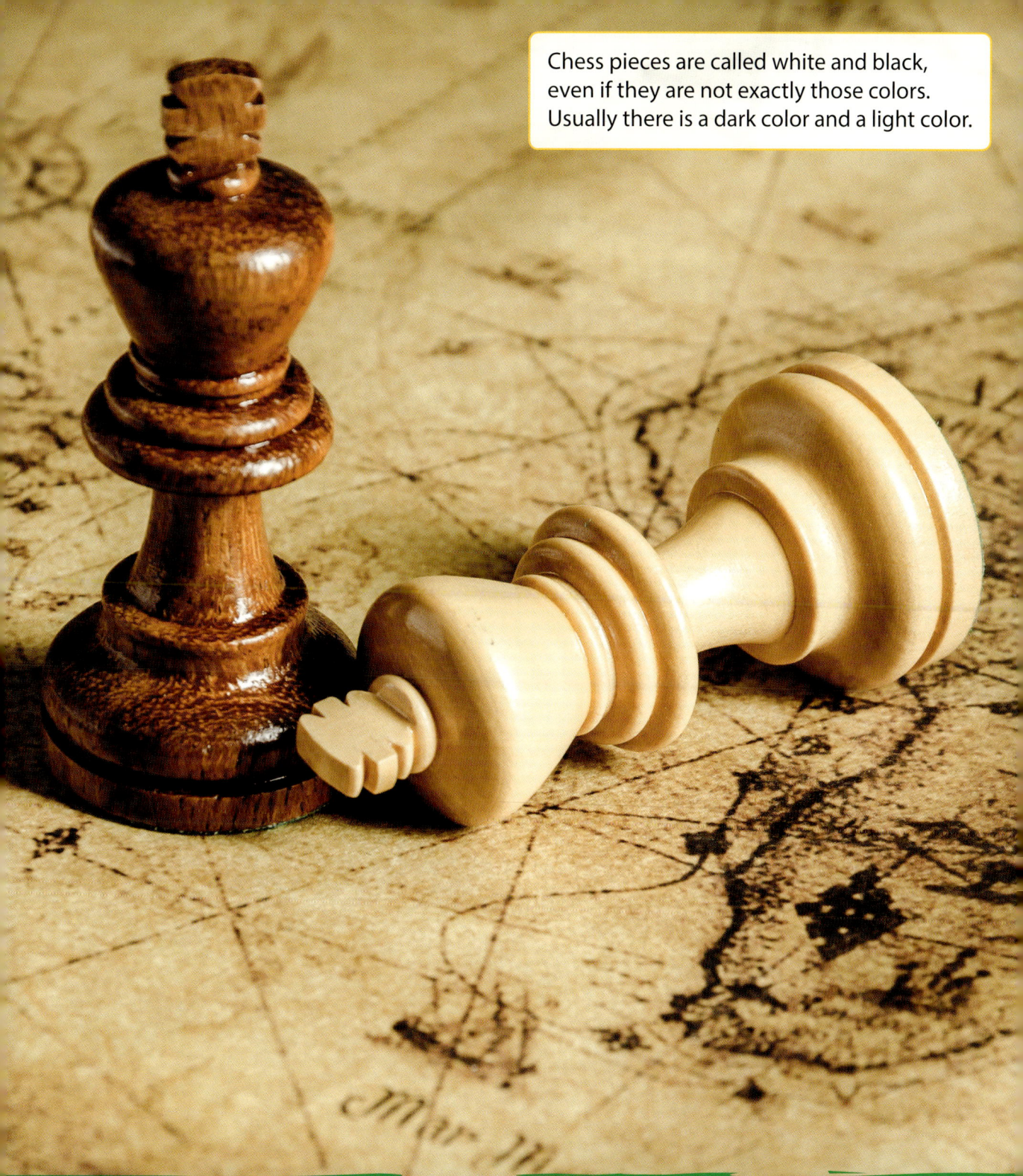

Chess Basics

Europeans gave chess pieces the names we know them by today. Each piece is a lesson in medieval history.

Pawns represent workers. Each player has eight pawns. There are more pawns than any other piece on the board. But they are also the weakest. Pawns are usually sacrificed to save more valuable pieces. They can move two squares forward on their first move. After that, they can usually only move forward one square at a time. Pawns can't go backward. They also can't jump over or move around other pieces. Pawns can capture pieces, but only if they are one square away diagonally.

Castle-shaped pieces represent a king and queen's castle. They are called rooks. The rook pieces originally represented **chariots**. They can move forward, backward, and side to side.

DID YOU KNOW?

White pieces always move first.
This wasn't an official rule until 1880.

Chessboard layout

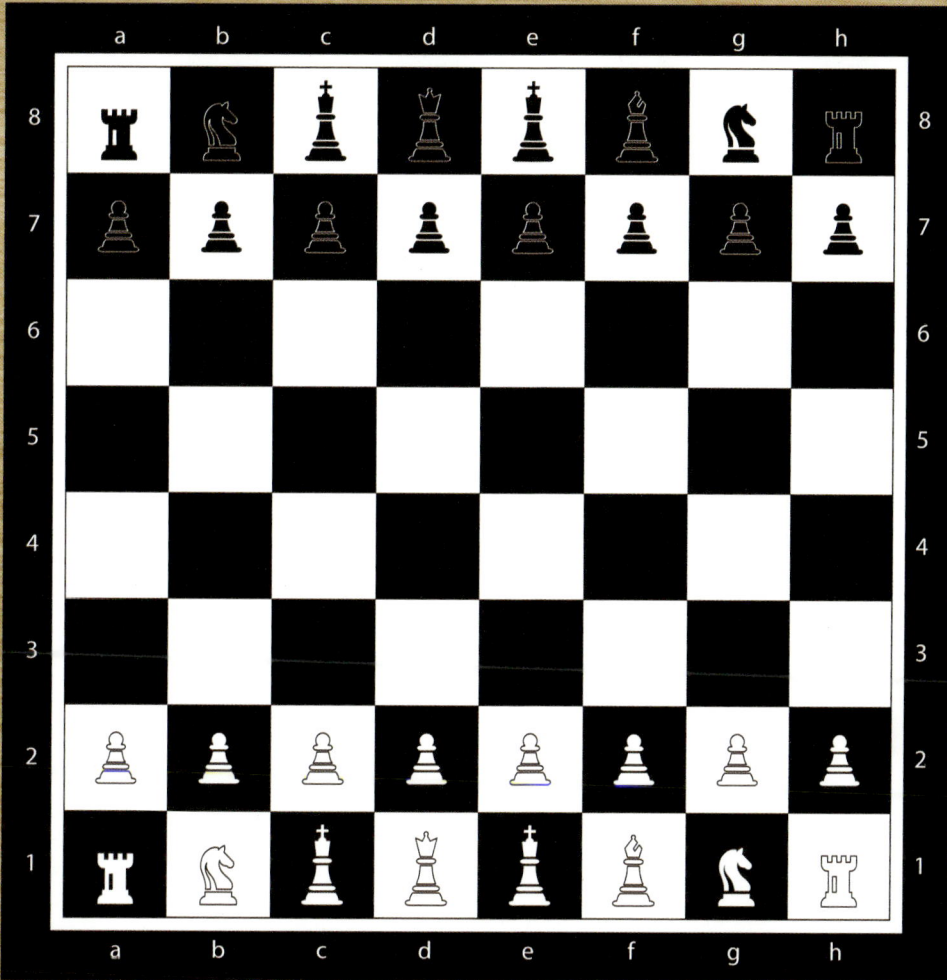

 Pawn

 Rook

 Bishop

 Knight

 King

Queen

Some players announce when they threaten their opponent with "check." Announcing "check" is not a rule, though.

Two knights are horse-shaped pieces. They protect the castles, king, and queen. Knights move in an L shape—two squares one way, and then one square over. They can leap over other pieces, like real horses.

Bishops are placed directly to the sides of the king and queen. In medieval times, religious leaders like bishops were powerful.

Each player has a queen. Queens can move in any direction. They can also move as far as they want, as long as no pieces are in the way. They are the most powerful piece on the board.

The king is less powerful than the queen, but it is the most important piece in the game. Kings can move one space in any direction. When the king is under attack, it is in "**check**." When one player's king cannot move anymore without being captured, it is a checkmate. The game is over.

The Father of Chess Theory

Francois-Andre Philidor was a French music **composer**. He was also considered to be the top chess player for 50 years. Some people call him the father of chess theory. In 1749, he published *Analysis of Chess*. It was the first book to thoroughly explain chess theory.

There are three parts to playing chess: the opening, the middlegame, and the endgame. Each part has its own way of thinking. Studying the game is called chess theory.

In the opening, players decide which pieces to bring into play, and when. The middlegame is when strategies are made and plans are worked out. The endgame begins once pieces have been exchanged.

Players watch other people play chess to study chess theory. They also read books. The first book on chess theory was written in 1620. No sport has had more books written about it than chess.

Grandmasters

There are more than 600 million chess players around the world. At any given time, there are only around 1,500–1,700 grandmasters. *Grandmaster* is the highest title a chess player can earn. International grandmasters earn their titles by playing against other grandmasters and international grandmasters. There are about 3,800 international grandmasters.

To be earned, each title has certain qualifications that must be met. The FIDE has awarded these titles since its founding. Earning a grandmaster title is the most difficult. Russia, the United States, China, India, and Ukraine are the top five countries for grandmasters.

A single person playing against multiple opponents is called a simultaneous exhibition, or "simul." Usually a grandmaster plays against multiple lower-ranked players.

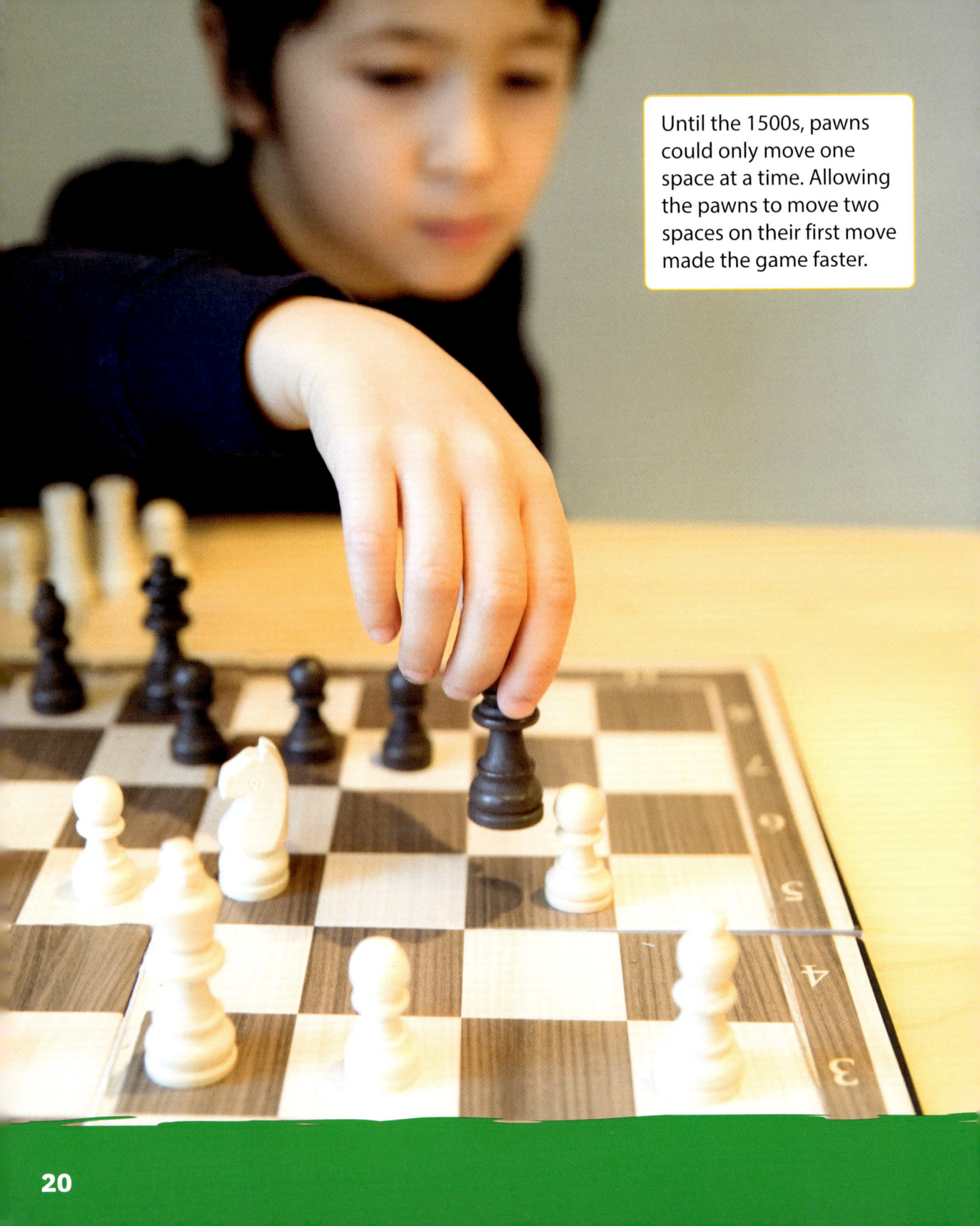

Until the 1500s, pawns could only move one space at a time. Allowing the pawns to move two spaces on their first move made the game faster.

A game that is hundreds of years old changes over time. Rules are updated. Until the 1300s, one of the ways a game could be won was to capture all the opponent's pieces. Until the 1400s, the queen was one of the weakest pieces. It could only go two spaces on its first move. After that, it could only move diagonally one space per turn!

There are also special moves. Castling is one of the most well-known moves. To castle, the king moves two spaces to the right or left. The rook moves to the square the king has just crossed. Castling moves the king to a safer place on the board. It also moves the rook closer to the opponent's king.

En passant is a move only pawns can do. Imagine that a white pawn has moved forward three spaces. On the next move, black moves the pawn in the next row over ahead two spaces. The white and black pawns are now next to each other. On its next move, the white pawn can capture the black pawn by moving diagonally. It is as though it had only moved one space instead of two.

DID YOU KNOW?

A player cannot castle if the king or its rook has moved. Castling can also not be done if the king is in check.

The longest recorded chess match lasted 20 hours, 15 minutes. With chess clocks, games are much shorter! Chess clocks are two connected clocks. One clock runs while player one decides on a move. The player makes a move. Then they stop the clock. The second clock starts as soon as the first clock stops. The first chess clock was used in 1883, at the London International Tournament.

Clocks limit the length of the game. The play time depends on the level of the players and the game type. The number of moves is also limited. All major FIDE events have a set time limit. Players have 90 minutes to make the first 40 moves. After that, an extra 30 minutes can be added to the game. Each player is granted 30 seconds per move. **Blitz chess** games are fast! They can be over in as little as three minutes.

Chess is a game of courtesy. Players should respect their opponent's time and give them their full attention. In 2009, Hou Yifan was five seconds late to a round of the Chinese Chess Championship. She was **disqualified**. If a player's phone goes off during a match, they lose automatically as well.

DID YOU KNOW?

The shortest game of chess lasted only two minutes! The **sequence** of moves is called Fool's Mate. Black is the only one who can win this way. The shortest game of chess between two grandmasters ended in four moves.

The British Chess Championship began in 1904. Until 2004, any player part of the British Commonwealth could enter. Guianan player JAM Osborn participated in 1935.

The Chess Community

Chess has always been a competition. In 1843, Englishman Howard Staunton beat French chess master Pierre Saint-Amant. Staunton was considered the world champion, even though a formal title did not yet exist.

The first modern chess game as we know it today was recorded in 1475. But the first international tournament was not held until 1851. It took place in London, England. Staunton helped plan it. He also made it to the semi-final round. But Adolf Anderssen won. Anderssen was the first international chess champion.

The first Chess Olympiad was held in July 1927. Sixteen countries sent players to London that year. Today the Olympiad is held every two years. More than 3,000 people compete. The 2020 event was delayed until 2021. But an online Chess Olympiad was held instead. Teams from 163 countries participated.

DID YOU KNOW?

The online Chess Olympiad in 2020 was a mixed event. The six-person teams were required to have at least three female players. They also needed to have at least two players under 20 years old.

Judit Polgár was the top woman in chess for 26 years, from 1989 to 2015.

The Women's Chess Association of America was formed in 1894. But women have only played against men at major events since the late 1980s. Only one out of every 15 players is a woman. There has never been a female world champion. But that doesn't mean there aren't great female chess players!

Judit Polgár is one of the strongest female players of all time. She is the only woman to hit the world's top 10. "It's not a matter of **gender**," she said. "It's a matter of being smart."

There is only one woman in the world's top 100 right now. Hou Yifan is a four-time world champion. She is also the highest-rated woman player in the world. In 2006, she played her first Women's World Championship. She was only 12 years old. She won four championships after that. And she was the youngest female grandmaster when she was 14.

DID YOU KNOW?

American grandmaster Jennifer Shahade has won two US Women's Chess Championships. She writes books busting **myths** about female players. She hopes to bring more girls into the world of chess.

Should there be separate events and titles for men and women? Players aren't sure. FIDE awards four women-specific titles, including female grandmaster. Earning these titles requires a lower rating than earning regular titles. Many women feel this makes the women's titles seem less important. It also limits how high they might aim. Chess players want to play to be the best player, not just the best female player.

Women-only events have smaller prizes. The press is less likely to cover the events. However, these events are places where female players can meet. Programs focusing on girls and women have more participation than mixed gender programs. And entry fees into tournaments cost less for women who hold FIDE titles.

The Gender Gap

There has never been a female world champion of chess. But that doesn't mean it's not possible. As with science and math careers, there is a gender gap. Females traditionally have not been encouraged to pursue these areas in the way males are. The same has historically been true about chess. But, female chess masters around the world want to change that. They are encouraging young girls and women to play to win. And young players are listening. In the early 2000s, only around 1 percent of players were women. Today, they make up nearly 15 percent of all players.

In 2014, Sarah Chiang (left) was the highest-ranked female player under the age of 21.

There are permanent chess tables and boards for people to play on all around New York City.

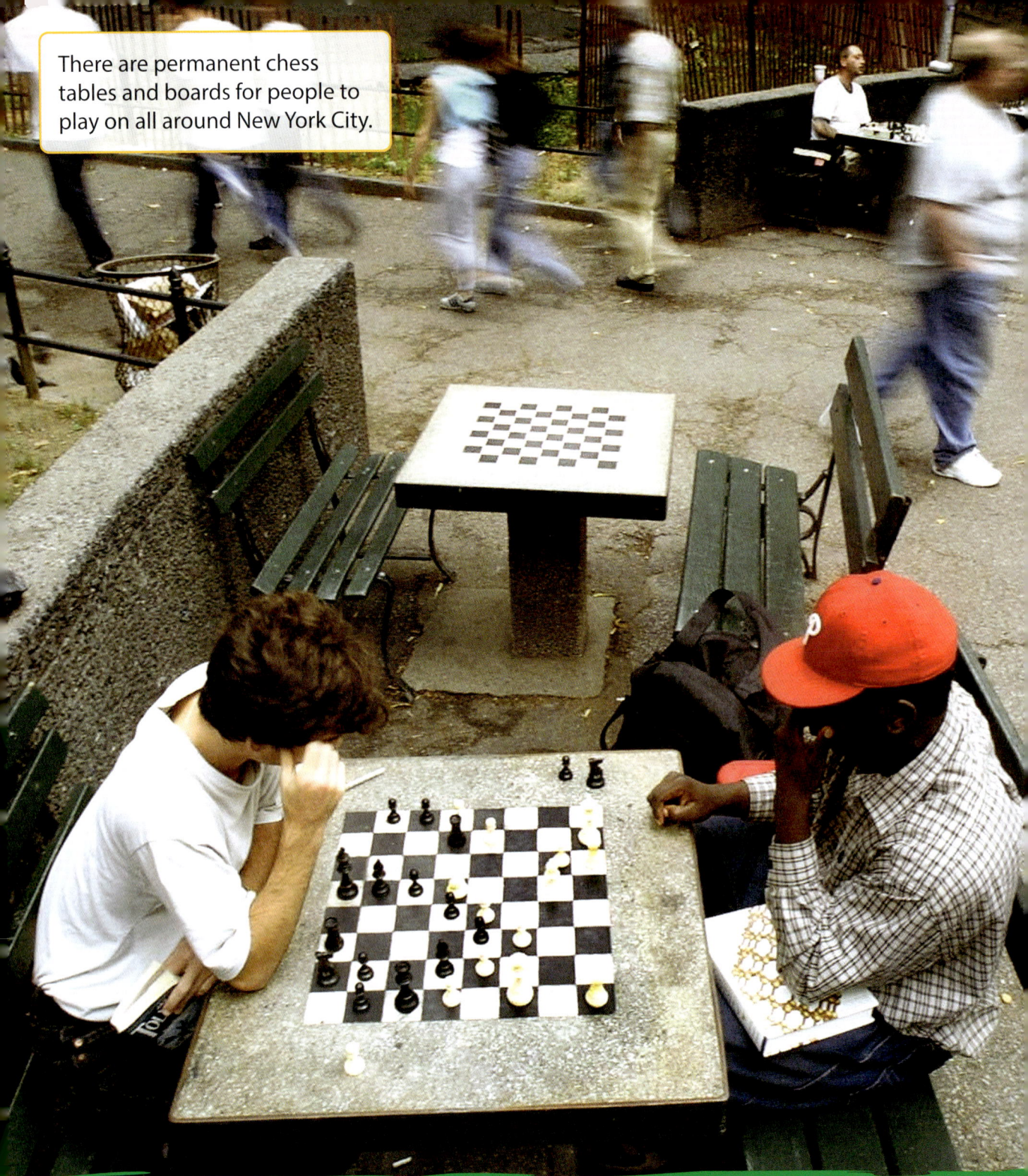

Grandmaster, international grandmaster, world champion…what if you just want to play? There are plenty of chances for players who aren't professionals!

New York City's chess in the park is famous. There are permanent chess tables in Washington Square and Union Square Parks. Chess masters bring boards and clocks. For $5, passersby can stop and play a game. Some chess masters offer lessons too.

There are pickup chess sites all over the world. Visitors can play a casual game on the street or in cafés. Cities like Copenhagen, Denmark; Berlin, Germany; Mexico City, Mexico; and Edinburgh, Scotland, all have public places to play.

Meet Me in the Park

Every year, the New York City parks department partners with Chess in the Schools to hold the Chess-in-the-Park Rapid Open in Central Park. In 2019, 775 players participated. There was something for everyone. International chess master Yury Lapshun accepted challengers all day. Beginners got to try Learn Chess with Dr. Wolf, an app that coaches new players through games.

Millions of kids play chess all over the world. It is a great way to develop a better memory. It makes kids smarter thinkers and better problem-solvers. Some countries are teaching it to everyone! In 2011, Armenian kids learned chess in school from ages six to eight. Many grandmasters come from Armenia.

In the United States, schools introduce more than 250,000 kids to chess every year. There are chess clubs, after-school programs, camps, and school tournaments.

In 2021, FIDE held the first Intercontinental ChessKid FIDE Challenge. It was open to players under 12 years old. More than 1,900 kids from 86 countries competed in the online tournament.

What's with Russia?

Before the Russian Revolution in 1917, only members of the elite society were allowed to play chess. By the 1920s, everyone was playing. They opened chess schools and held tournaments. Then hundreds of thousands of people could learn and play. Russia still dominates the sport today.

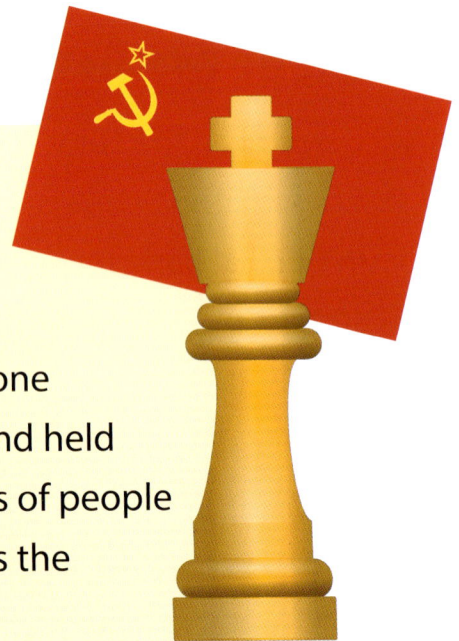

Playing chess can help kids build better puzzle and problem-solving skills.

The Future of Chess

Chess has been around for hundreds of years. It will likely be around for hundreds more. Movies like *Searching for Bobby Fischer* make famous players household names. In 2017, chess master Magnus Carlsen was a guest on *The Simpsons*. *The Queen's Gambit* gave people a view into the world of women in chess.

In 2019, FIDE pushed to get chess added to the 2024 Paris Olympic Games. Four new events, including skateboard and surfing, were added in 2020. Fans hoped chess would be the next new sport. Unfortunately, it failed. They still hope to add it to a future Olympics.

DID YOU KNOW?

International Chess Day is on July 20. It commemorates the day FIDE was founded in 1924.

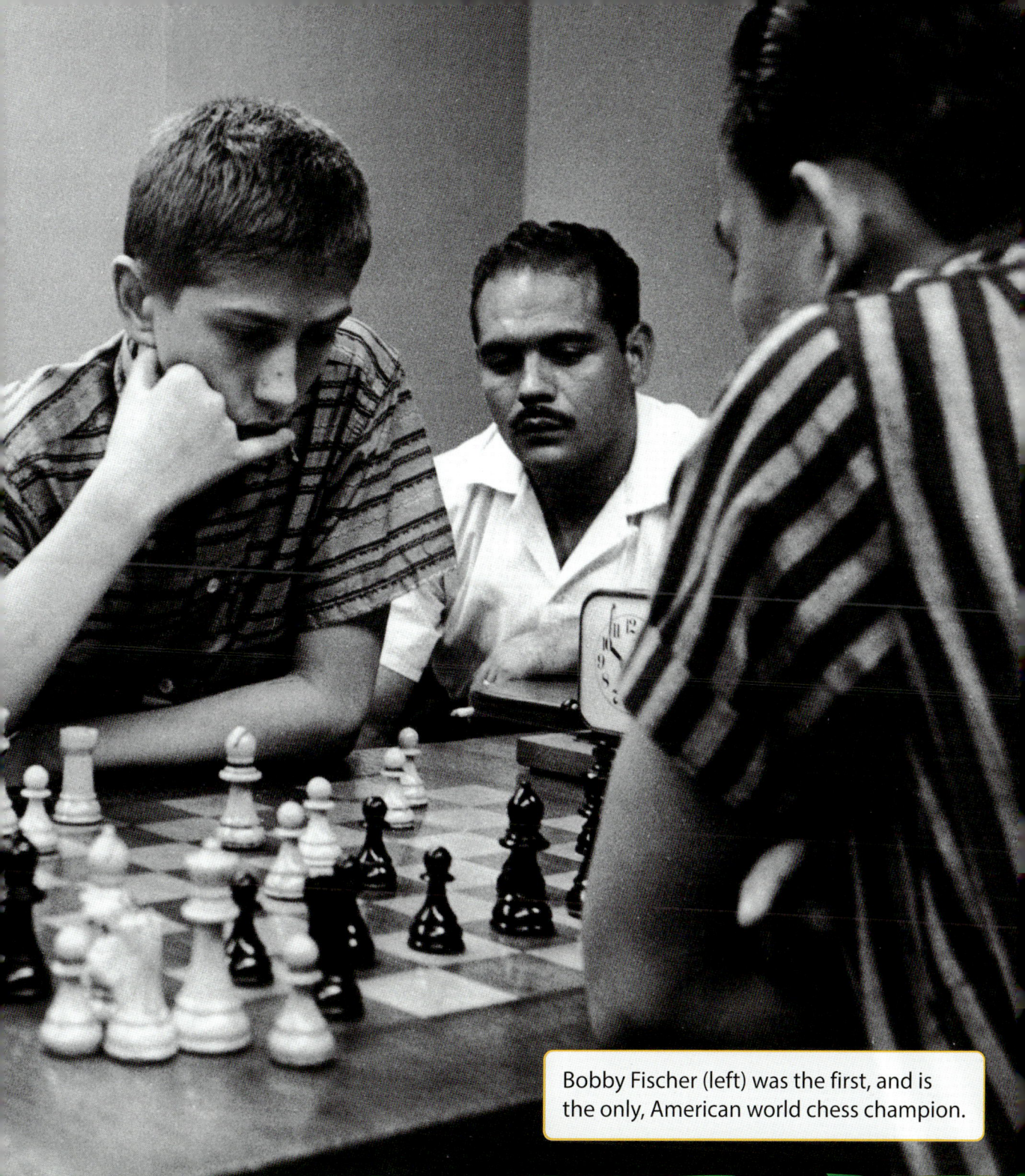

Bobby Fischer (left) was the first, and is the only, American world chess champion.

Grandmaster Hikaru Nakamura posed in front of the largest chess piece in the world.

As of 2020, more than 17 million games of chess are played online every day. There are also other chess websites and apps for players. But people don't just like playing chess. They also like watching it.

Twitch is the world's leading **streaming** service for gamers. Fans tune in to watch gamers play Minecraft, Fortnite, and Among Us. But chess is a popular game to watch too! Two of the 10 most popular streamers are women. The top chess streamer is Hikaru Nakamura. He is an American grandmaster and five-time US chess champion.

In 2021, Twitch and Chess.com teamed up. They held a series of chess tournaments called PogChamps. Top non-chess streamers and internet personalities joined in. They competed for hundreds of thousands of dollars in prize money.

DID YOU KNOW?

The COVID-19 pandemic gave chess streaming a huge boost in 2020. People were home more. They needed new things to watch. Viewers watched more than 41 million hours of chess between March and August. This was four times more than the previous six months.

Chess is a sport for everyone. It can be played between two people of any age, size, physical ability, gender, financial background, or skill. People from different countries could play without speaking the same language. Chess sets can be adapted for players with physical or visual handicaps. In 2020, FIDE held its first online Chess Olympiad. It was for players with disabilities. More than 400 players, including two grandmasters, took part.

A chess set can be found for less than $10. Small sets can be carried anywhere. And these days, matches can be played online.

DID YOU KNOW?

US chess members are given ratings based on their results in official tournaments. Ratings start at 100 and go up to 3,000.

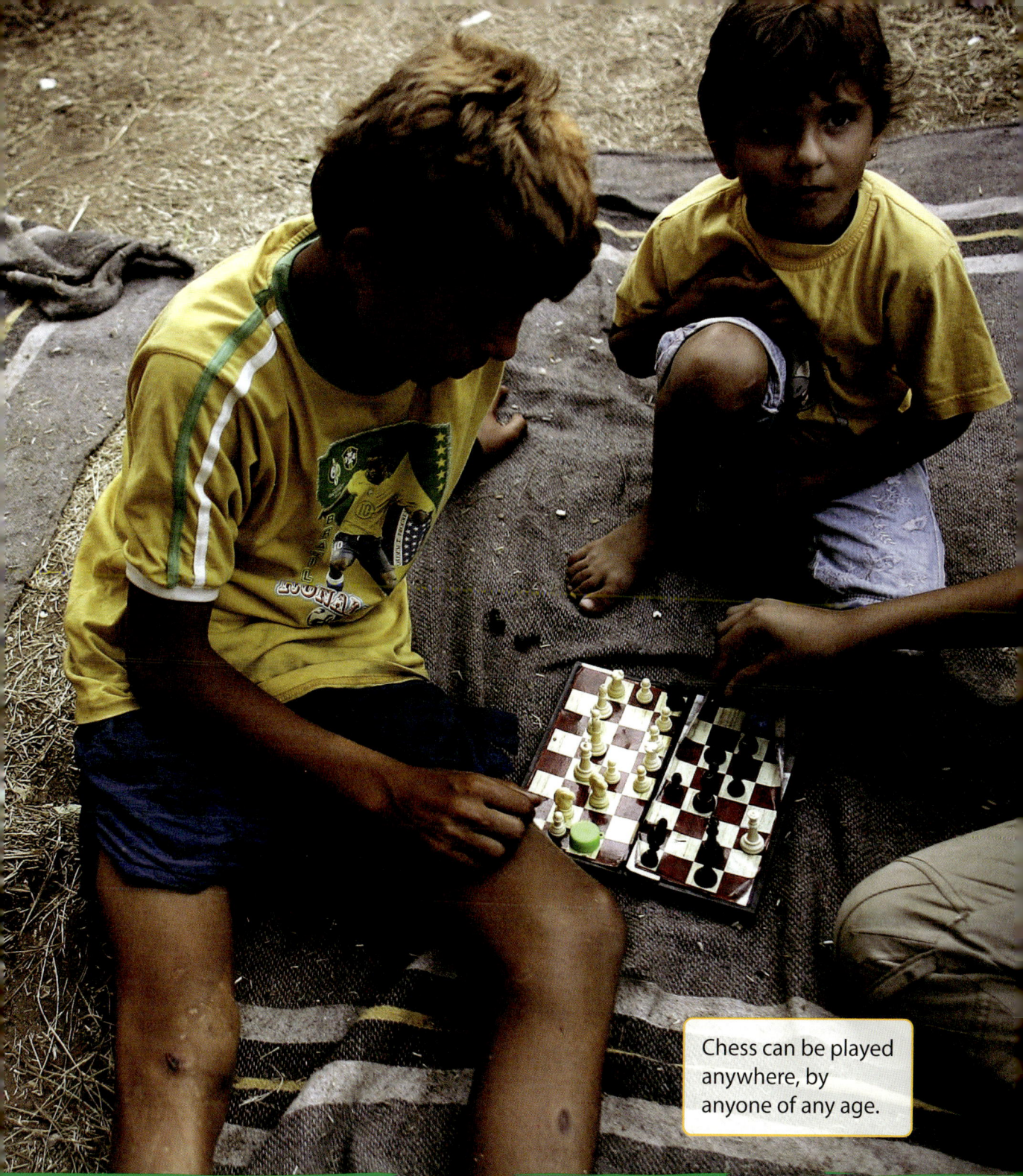

Chess can be played anywhere, by anyone of any age.

In 2003, Garry Kasparov played a rematch against Deep Junior, a scaled-down version of Deep Blue. The match ended in a tie, with each winning three games.

GARRY KA

There is more than one way to play chess! There are thousands of variants. Variants are games related to, or inspired by, chess. There is at least one major difference from the original game. Some versions have pairs of players. Another version places all the non-pawns in random positions.

In the late 1970s, digital chessboards entered the market. Players would enter their move with a keypad. A computer would print out its move or show the move on a display. Then the player would place the pieces for each side on the board.

In the mid-1980s, IBM built a chess-playing computer called Deep Blue. In 1996, it played a six-game match against grandmaster Garry Kasparov. Kasparov is considered the greatest chess player of all time. Deep Blue only won one of the six games. But they played a rematch in 1997. This time, Deep Blue was the winner.

DID YOU KNOW?

The most expensive chess set is called the Pearl Royale. It is made of solid white gold and covered in diamonds, sapphires, and pearls. The set is worth $4 million.

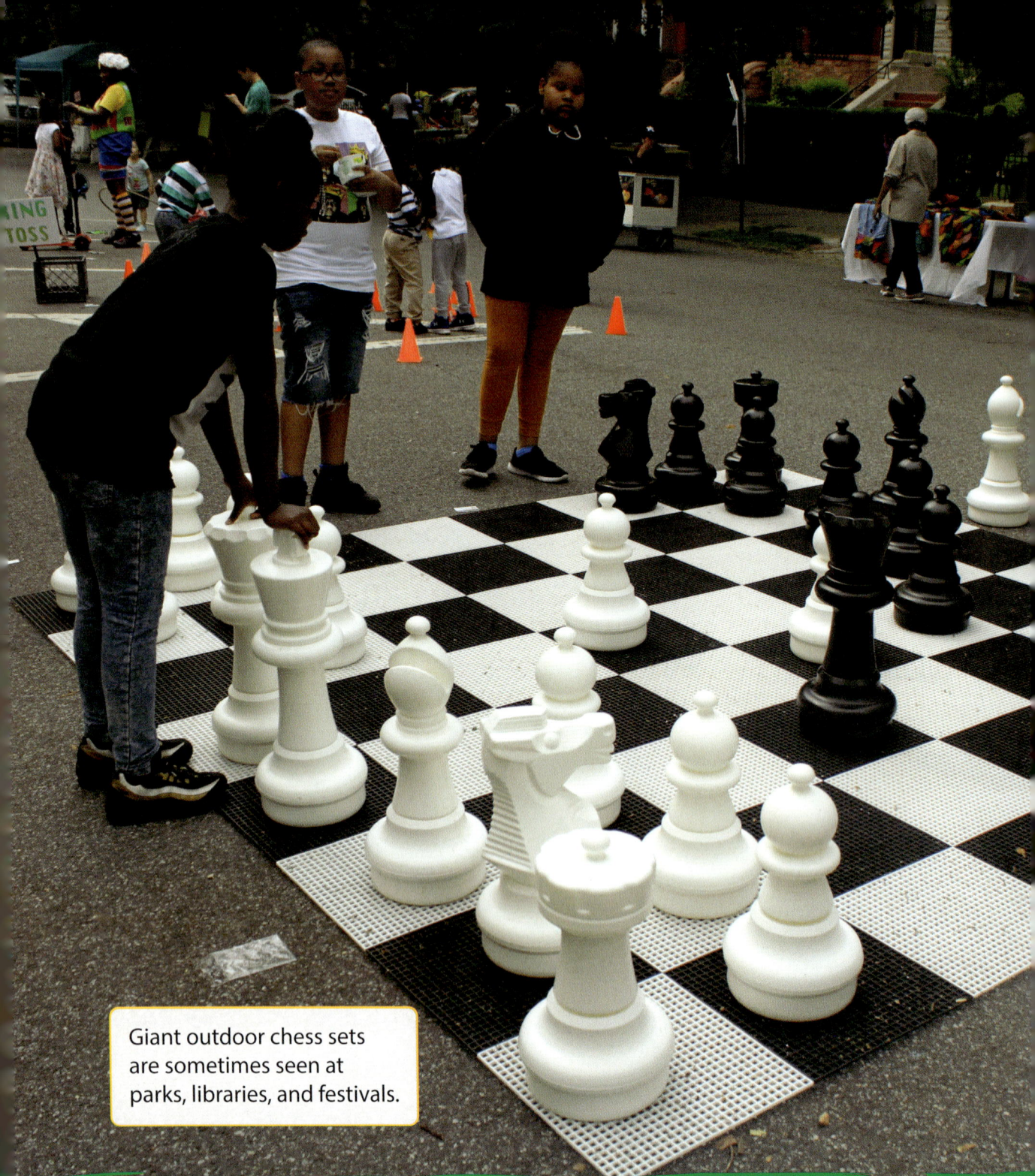

Giant outdoor chess sets are sometimes seen at parks, libraries, and festivals.

Today people can buy chess sets that show off their personalities. Nintendo, the Muppets, LEGO, and Star Trek all make chess sets. Some people try to collect them all. The owner of the world's largest chess collection has 412 sets!

Chess is huge in more than one way! The largest chess piece in the world stands in front of the World Chess Hall of Fame in St. Louis, Missouri. It is 20 feet (6 meters) tall. The smallest handmade set is tinier than a dime.

The game of chess has something for everyone. Games can stretch on for days or be as short as a minute. They can be played with friends online and in person. Whether players stick to tradition or make their own rules, there is something for everyone.

Playing a Real Game Online

The Wizard's Chess game in *Harry Potter* inspired an inventor to create a smart board game. Players can connect with opponents around the world through an app. The app sends moves to the board, and the board moves the pieces on its own.

Glossary

blitz chess: a game of extremely fast chess

chariots: two-wheeled horse-drawn carts

check: a condition in chess that occurs when a player's king is under threat of being captured during their opponent's next turn

checkmate: the capture of a player's king, ending the game

chess theory: the study of chess

composer: someone who writes music

disqualified: removed from a competition for breaking the rules

gender: the state of being male or female

grandmasters: chess players of the highest level

myths: widely held but false beliefs or ideas

sequence: a set of movements that are connected

streaming: viewing over a computer network

For More Information

Books

Basman, Michael. *Chess for Kids.* New York: Dorling Kindersley Pub., 2001. Written by an international grandmaster, this book teaches readers the rules, skills, and techniques to play the game.

Lombardy, William. *Chess for Children, Step by Step: A New, Easy Way to Learn the Game.* New York: Ishi Press International, 2018. This book introduces kids to the game of chess, using a series of games to help players understand each piece.

Websites

Chess.com This is a place for people to play chess puzzles, lessons, and games, connect with other players, and get the latest chess news.

Chesskid.com This website teaches kids how to play chess and helps parents and coaches teach chess.

Index

About the Author

Marissa Bolte has worked in publishing as a writer and editor for more than 15 years. She has written dozens of books about things like science and craft projects, historical figures and events, and pop culture. She lives in Minnesota.